ROMEO *and* JULIET

Shakespeare
THE ANIMATED TALES
ROMEO and JULIET

ABRIDGED BY LEON GARFIELD

ILLUSTRATED BY IGOR MAKAROV

HEINEMANN YOUNG BOOKS

Shakespeare The Animated Tales is a multinational venture conceived by S4C, Channel 4 Wales. Produced in Russia, Wales and England, the series has been financed by S4C, the BBC and HIT Communications (UK), Christmas Films and Soyuzmultfilm (Russia), Home Box Office (USA) and Fujisankei (Japan).

Academic Panel
Professor Stanley Wells
Dr Rex Gibson

Academic Co-ordinator
Roy Kendall

Educational Adviser
Michael Marland

Publishing Editor and Co-ordinator
Jane Fior

Book Design
Fiona Macmillan

Animation Director for *Romeo and Juliet*
Efim Gambourg of Soyuzmultfilm Studios, Moscow

Series Producer and Director
Dave Edwards of The Dave Edwards Studio Ltd, Cardiff

Executive Producers
Christopher Grace
Elizabeth Babakhina

William Heinemann Ltd
Michelin House, 81 Fulham Road
London SW3 6RB
LONDON · MELBOURNE · AUCKLAND
First published 1992
Text and illustrations © Shakespeare Animated Films Limited
and Christmas Joint Venture 1992
ISBN 0 434 96234 1
Printed and bound in the UK by BPCC Hazell Books Limited

The publishers would like to thank Paul Cox for
the use of his illustration of The Globe and
the series logo illustration, Carole Kempe for
her calligraphy, Patrick Spottiswoode for his
introduction and Elizabeth Laird, Ness Wood,
Rosa Fior and Jillian Boothroyd for their help
in the production of the books.

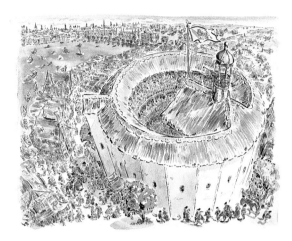

THE THEATRE IN SHAKESPEARE'S DAY

IN 1989 AN ARCHAEOLOGICAL discovery was made on the south bank of the Thames that sent shivers of delight through the theatre world. A fragment of Shakespeare's own theatre, the Globe, where many of his plays were first performed, had been found.

This discovery has fuelled further interest in how Shakespeare himself conceived and staged his plays. We know a good deal already, and archaeology as well as documentary research will no doubt reveal more, but although we can only speculate on some of the details, we have a good idea of what the Elizabethan theatre-goer saw, heard and smelt when he went to see a play by William Shakespeare at the Globe.

It was an entirely different experience from anything we know today. Modern theatres have roofs to keep out the weather. If it rained on the Globe, forty per cent of the play-goers got wet. Audiences today sit on cushioned seats, and usually (especially if the play is by Shakespeare) watch and listen in respectful silence. In the Globe, the floor of the theatre was packed with a riotous crowd of garlic-reeking apprentices, house servants and artisans, who had each paid a penny to stand for the entire duration of the play, to buy nuts and apples from the food-sellers, to refresh themselves with bottled ale, relieve themselves, perhaps, into buckets by the back wall, to talk, cheer, catcall, clap and hiss if the play did not please them.

In the galleries, that rose in curved tiers around the inside of the building, sat those who could afford to pay two pennies for a seat, and the benefits of a roof over their heads. Here, the middle ranking citizens, the merchants, the sea captains, the clerks from the Inns of Court, would sit crammed into their small eighteen inch space and look down upon the 'groundlings' below. In the 'Lords room', the rich and the great, noblemen and women, courtiers and foreign ambassadors had to pay sixpence each for the relative comfort and luxury of their exclusive position directly above the stage, where they smoked tobacco, and overlooked the rest.

We are used to a stage behind an arch, with wings on either side, from which the actors come on and into which they disappear. In the Globe, the stage was a platform thrusting out into the middle of the floor, and the audience, standing in the central yard, surrounded it on three sides. There were no wings. Three doors at the back of the stage were used for all exits and entrances. These were sometimes covered by a curtain, which could be used as a prop.

Today we sit in a darkened theatre or cinema, and look at a brilliantly lit stage or screen, or we sit at home in a small, private world of our own, watching a luminous television screen. The close-packed, rowdy crowd at the Globe, where the play started at two o'clock in the afternoon, had no artificial light to enhance their illusion. It was the words that moved them. They came to listen, rather than to see.

No dimming lights announced the start of the play. A blast from a trumpet and three sharp knocks warned the audience that the action was about to begin. In the broad daylight, the actor could see the audience as clearly as the audience could see him. He spoke directly to the crowd, and held them with his eyes, following their reactions. He could play up to the raucous laughter that greeted the comical, bawdy scenes, and gauge the emotional response to the higher flights of poetry. Sometimes he even improvised speeches of his own. He was surrounded by, enfolded by his audience.

The stage itself would seem uncompromisingly bare to our eyes. There was no scenery. No painted backdrops suggested a forest, or a castle, or the sumptuous interior of a palace. Shakespeare painted the scenery with his words, and the imagination of the audience did the rest.

Props were brought onto the stage only when they were essential for the action. A bed would be carried on when a character needed to lie on it. A throne would be let down from above when a king needed to sit on it. Torches and lanterns would suggest that it was dark, but the main burden of persuading an audience, at three o'clock in the afternoon, that it was in fact the middle of the night, fell upon the language.

Some of the loveliest references to the night appear in *Romeo and Juliet*. Romeo says: 'O she doth teach the torches to burn bright. It seems she hangs upon the cheek of night as a rich jewel in an Ethiop's ear.'

Shakespeare's actors were responsible for their own costumes. They would use what was to hand in the 'tiring house' (dressing room), or supplement it out of their own pockets. Classical, medieval and Tudor clothes could easily appear side by side in the same play.

No women actors appeared on a public stage until many years after Shakespeare's death, for at that time it would have been considered shameless. The parts of young girls were played by boys. The parts of older women were played by older men.

In 1613 the Globe theatre was set on fire by a spark from a cannon during a performance of Henry VIII, and it burnt to the ground. The actors, including Shakespeare himself, dug into their own pockets and paid for it to be rebuilt. The new theatre lasted until 1642, when it closed again. Now, in the 1990s, the Globe is set to rise again as a committed band of actors, scholars and enthusiasts are raising the money to rebuild Shakespeare's theatre in its original form a few yards from its previous site.

From the time when the first Globe theatre was built until today, Shakespeare's plays have been performed in a vast variety of languages, styles, costumes and techniques, on stage, on film, on television and in animated film. Shakespeare himself, working within the round wooden walls of his theatre, would have been astonished by it all.

Patrick Spottiswoode
Director Globe Education,
Shakespeare Globe Trust

WILLIAM SHAKESPEARE

NEXT TO GOD, A wise man once said, Shakespeare created most. In the thirty-seven plays that are his chief legacy to the world—and surely no-one ever left a richer!—human nature is displayed in all its astonishing variety.

He has enriched the stage with matchless comedies, tragedies, histories, and, towards the end of his life, with plays that defy all description, strange plays that haunt the imagination like visions.

His range is enormous: kings and queens, priests, princes and merchants, soldiers, clowns and drunkards, murderers, pimps, whores, fairies, monsters and pale, avenging ghosts 'strut and fret their hour upon the stage'. Murders and suicides abound; swords flash, blood flows, poison drips, and lovers sigh; yet there is always time for old men to talk of growing apples and for gardeners to discuss the weather.

In the four hundred years since they were written, they have become known and loved in every land; they are no longer the property of one country and one people, they are the priceless possession of the world.

His life, from what we know of it, was not astonishing. The stories that have attached themselves to him are remarkable only for their ordinariness: poaching deer, sleeping off a drinking bout under a wayside tree. There are no duels, no loud, passionate loves, no excesses of any kind. He was not one of your unruly geniuses whose habits are more interesting than their works. From all accounts, he was of a gentle, honourable disposition, a good businessman, and a careful father.

He was born on April 23rd 1564, to John and Mary Shakespeare of Henley Street, Stratford-upon-Avon. He was their third child and first son. When he was four or five he began his education at the local petty school. He left the local grammar school when he was about fourteen, in all probability to help in his father's glove-making shop. When he was eighteen, he married Anne Hathaway, who lived in a nearby village. By the time he was twenty-one, he was the father of three children, two daughters and a son.

Then, it seems, a restless mood came upon him. Maybe he travelled, maybe he was, as some say, a schoolmaster in the country; but at some time during the next seven years, he went to London and found employment in the theatre. When he was twenty-eight, he was already well enough known as an actor and playwright to excite the spiteful envy of a rival, who referred to him as 'an upstart crow'.

He mostly lived and worked in London until his mid-forties, when he returned to his family and home in Stratford, where he remained in prosperous circumstances until his death on April 23rd 1616, his fifty-second birthday.

He left behind him a widow, two daughters (his son died in childhood), and the richest imaginary world ever created by the human mind.

ROMEO AND JULIET

This is the most famous love story in the world. Set in old Verona, where streets were narrow, walls were high and the sun was hot, and young men, bright as wasps, wore swords for their stings, it tells of a pair of lovers destroyed by the hatred of their rival families.

Shakespeare wrote it when he was about thirty-one. He took the story from a well-known poem of the time, and transformed it from a dull piece into a glittering marvel. Glittering is indeed the word: the play radiates light … not the light of the sun, but light that shines in darkness: torches, moon, stars and the lovers themselves. When Romeo first sees Juliet he declares, 'She doth teach the torches to burn bright', and when Juliet dreams of Romeo, she sighs, 'when he shall die, take him and cut him out in little stars, and he will make the face of heaven so fine that all the world will be in love with night.'

Although it is a tragedy, it is a play of almost as much laughter as tears; although it is a love story, it is a play of as many quarrels as kisses and as much fury as tenderness in its brief journey from the bedchamber to the tomb.

Some critics have complained that the play is no true tragedy, as the disaster that overwhelms the young lovers is brought about by chance – a letter that miscarries – and so is artificial and contrived. But this is not so. The tragedy is implicit from the very outset. Before Romeo sets eyes on Juliet, he has a premonition of ill-fortune, and when Juliet sees Romeo in the night she fancies him a dead man in a tomb; and even the kindly priest who marries them warns: 'These violent delights have violent ends, and in their triumph die.'

A tragic end is essential to Shakespeare's design. He tells the story of first love—a love so sudden, so bright, so intense that it cannot last. It is, as Juliet says, 'too like the lightning, that doth cease to be ere one can say it lightens.'

Had the lovers lived on, at best their bright flame would have sunk to a cosy glow; at worst, it would have turned to bitter ashes or mere forgetfulness. Death alone could preserve it in all its 'feasting presence full of light'. Life would have destroyed it; death has kept it bright for ever.

LEON GARFIELD

The Characters in the Play

in order of appearance

BENVOLIO	*Montague's nephew, friend to Romeo and Mercutio*
TYBALT	*Lady Capulet's nephew*
A CITIZEN	
CAPULET	*head of a Veronese family, at feud with the Montagues*
LADY CAPULET	
MONTAGUE	*head of a Veronese family, at feud with the Capulets*
LADY MONTAGUE	
ESCALUS	*Prince of Verona*
ROMEO	*Montague's son*
SERVANT	*to the Capulets*
MERCUTIO	*a young gentleman, kinsman of the Prince, friend of Romeo*
SERVANT	*at the masked ball*
JULIET	*Capulet's daughter*
NURSE	*a Capulet servant, Juliet's foster-mother*
FRIAR LAURENCE	*of the Franciscan order*
SERVANT	*of Romeo*
APOTHECARY	*of Mantua*
FRIAR JOHN	*of the Franciscan order*

The curtain rises on old Verona, on a market-place covered over with huge umbrella-awnings that shield the busy crowded stalls from the blazing summer's sun. All of a sudden, the umbrellas quake and tumble aside to reveal, like furious insects under a stone, a frantic squabbling of mad colours. Shouts and shrieks fill the air, of fright and rage and outrage! The Montagues and the Capulets—two ancient warring families—are at each others' throats again! Stalls are wrecked, merchandise scattered and screaming children snatched out of the way by their terrified mothers.

VOICES   Down with the Capulets! Down with the Montagues!

Benvolio, a sensible young Montague, seeks to put an end to the uproar.

BENVOLIO   Part, fools, put up your swords!

He is accosted by Tybalt, a dangerous Capulet.

TYBALT   Turn thee, Benvolio, look upon thy death!

They fight, causing more destruction to all about them.

A CITIZEN   A plague on both your houses!

Old Capulet, venerable and dignified, accompanied by his wife and a servant, appears upon the scene. At once, the old man's heart is stirred into a fury.

CAPULET   Give me my long sword, ho!

LADY CAPULET   (*restraining him*) A crutch, a crutch! Why call you for a sword?

Too late. The old man has seen his chief enemy. Old Montague and his lady approach.

CAPULET   My sword, I say! Old Montague is come!

MONTAGUE   Thou villain Capulet!

He draws his sword, but Lady Montague drags him back.

MONTAGUE   Hold me not! Let me go!

LADY MONTAGUE Thou shalt not stir one foot to seek a foe!

Trumpets sound. Soldiers and Prince Escalus enter the market-place. Enraged by the scene of civil strife that greets him, the prince shouts, at first, in vain.

PRINCE   Rebellious subjects, enemies to peace—Will they not hear?
               What ho, you men, you beasts! On pain of torture, throw your

mistempered weapons to the ground and hear the sentence of your moved prince. (*The fighting ceases.*) Three civil brawls, bred of an airy word, by thee, old Capulet, and Montague, have thrice disturbed the quiet of our streets. If ever you disturb our streets again, your lives shall pay the forfeit of the peace. For this time all the rest depart away.

At the Prince's words the crowd obediently disperses, leaving ruin and the creators of it behind. Sternly, the Prince addresses the two old men.

PRINCE   You, Capulet, shall go along with me, and Montague, come you this afternoon, to know our farther pleasure in this case.

He turns and rides away. Old Capulet and his wife follow, and with them, the sullen Tybalt. Angrily, Lady Capulet snatches his rapier away from him, as if depriving a naughty child of its toy. Old Montague, his wife and Benvolio are left behind with a stall-keeper or two, crawling about to recover scattered possessions.

LADY MONTAGUE   O where is Romeo, saw you him today?

BENVOLIO   Madam, underneath the grove of sycamore did I see your son—

MONTAGUE   —Many a morning hath he there been seen, with tears augmenting the fresh morning's dew, adding to clouds more clouds with his deep sighs . . .

BENVOLIO   My noble uncle, do you know the cause?

MONTAGUE   I neither know it, nor can learn it of him.

BENVOLIO   See where he comes!

Enter Romeo, a sad figure, moving disconsolately along a colonnade. He pauses by a column and, with his dagger, begins to incise in the stone.

BENVOLIO   (*to Montague and his wife*) So please you step aside; I'll know his grievance or be much denied.

Old Montague and his wife depart. Benvolio approaches Romeo.

BENVOLIO   Good morrow, cousin.

ROMEO   (*obscuring his knife-work*) What, is the day so young?

BENVOLIO   But new struck nine.

ROMEO   Ay me, sad hours seem long.

BENVOLIO   What sadness lengthens Romeo's hours?

For answer, Romeo reveals what he has been hiding: the name, 'Rosalyne' with an added heart. All the columns he has passed have been similarly wounded by his loving dagger.

BENVOLIO	In love?
ROMEO	Out. Out of her favour where I am in love.

Benvolio seats himself upon a step, and signs to Romeo to join him.

BENVOLIO	Be ruled by me, forget to think of her.
ROMEO	O teach me how I should forget.
BENVOLIO	By giving liberty unto thine eyes: examine other beauties.
ROMEO	(*rising*) Farewell, thou canst not teach me—

As he speaks, a puzzled figure comes into the market-place. It is a servant of the Capulets. He is studying a piece of paper. It is a list of guests invited to a feast at his master's house. Unfortunately, he cannot read. He approaches Romeo.

SERVANT	I pray sir, can you read?
ROMEO	Ay, mine own fortune in my misery.
SERVANT	Perhaps you have learned it without book.

He turns to go. Romeo detains him.

ROMEO
Stay, fellow, I can read. (*He takes the paper and begins to read.*)

ROMEO
Signor Martino and his wife and daughters; County Anselm and his beauteous sisters; the lady widow of Utruvio; Signor Placentio and his lovely nieces; Mercutio and his brother Valentine; mine uncle Capulet, his wife and daughters; my fair niece Rosalyne— (*Romeo pauses, then reads on*) —and Livia; Signor Valentio and his cousin Tybalt; Lucio and the lively Helena. (*He returns the list.*) A fair assembly. Whither should they come?

SERVANT
My master is the great rich Capulet, and if you be not of the house of Montagues, I pray come and crush a cup of wine. Rest you merry.

The servant departs with the list.

BENVOLIO
At this same ancient feast of Capulet's sups the fair Rosalyne. Go thither and with unattainted eye compare her face with some that I shall show and I will make thee think thy swan a crow.

ROMEO
One fairer than my love! The all-seeing sun ne'er saw her match!

BENVOLIO
Tut, you saw her fair, none else being by . . .

The house of the Capulets is noisy with revelry. Gorgeous guests move to and fro. Masks, masks, masks! In black and silver, scarlet and gold: snarling beast-masks, beaked bird-masks, devil-masks, and masks as pale and blank as the moon . . . all shifting, turning, nodding, while through their black slits peep eyes that burn and sparkle and shoot voluptuous arrows of desire . . . Old Capulet, the host, bustles about in high delight.

CAPULET
Welcome, gentlemen, ladies that have their toes unplagued with corns will walk a bout with you . . . Come, musicians, play! A hall, a hall, give room! And foot it, girls!

A stately air strikes up. Couples form, beasts and moon-faces . . . By the door stand Romeo and Benvolio. Hastily, they don their masks. Romeo's is calm and golden . . . Benvolio tries to drag Romeo into the festivities. He will not come. Mercutio, Romeo's good friend and kinsman to the prince, in a mask that reflects his lively, mocking nature, joins them. He lays an affectionate arm round Romeo's shoulder.

MERCUTIO   We must have you dance!

ROMEO   Not I, believe me. You have dancing shoes with nimble soles; I have a soul of lead.

MERCUTIO   You are a lover; borrow Cupid's wings!

ROMEO   Peace, peace, Mercutio, peace. (*Mercutio shrugs his shoulders and moves away. Romeo murmurs to himself.*) My mind misgives some consequence yet hanging in the stars shall bitterly begin his fearful date with this night's revels . . .

He gazes at the dancers: a long procession of pale moon-faces linked with lascivious beasts. Suddenly one face is seen unmasked. It is the face of a young girl and it seems to flood the world with radiance. Romeo cries out in amazement. He turns to a servant beside him.

ROMEO   What lady's that which doth enrich the hand of yonder knight?

SERVANT   I know not, sir.

ROMEO   O she doth teach the torches to burn bright. It seems she hangs upon the cheek of night as a rich jewel in an Ethiop's ear! Did my heart love till now? Forswear it, sight, for I ne'er saw true beauty till this night!

He moves towards her like one in a dream. He passes close by Tybalt . . .

TYBALT   This by his voice should be a Montague! (*He turns to a serving-boy.*) Fetch me my rapier, boy! What, dares the slave come hither—

Old Capulet, seeing that Tybalt is enraged, approaches.

CAPULET   How now, kinsman, wherefore storm you so?

TYBALT   Uncle, this is a Montague, our foe!

CAPULET   Young Romeo, is it?

TYBALT   'Tis he, that villain Romeo.

CAPULET   Content thee, gentle coz, let him alone.

TYBALT   I'll not endure him!

CAPULET   He shall be endured! Go to, am I the master here or you? Go to, go to!

Old Capulet bustles away, leaving Tybalt to stare murderously towards Romeo. Romeo, unaware of the hostility he has aroused, has managed to obtain the unknown beauty as his partner in the dance. He takes her hand and holds up his mask.

ROMEO   If I profane with my unworthiest hand this holy shrine, the gentle sin is this, my lips, two blushing pilgrims, ready stand to smooth that rough touch with a tender kiss.

JULIET   Good pilgrim, you do wrong your hand too much, which mannerly devotion shows in this: saints have hands that pilgrims' hands do touch, and palm to palm is holy palmer's kiss.

ROMEO   Have not saints lips, and holy palmers too? (*Gently, and under the concealment of the mask, he kisses her.*) O trespass sweetly urged. Give me my sin again!

They kiss again.

JULIET   You kiss by th'book—

As they converse, lost in each other, Juliet's nurse, a busy, capacious dame approaches.

NURSE   —Madam— (*hastily, the lovers' faces fly apart*) —your mother craves a word with you.

Obediently, Juliet departs.

ROMEO   What is her mother?

NURSE   Marry, bachelor, her mother is the lady of the house. I nursed her daughter that you talked withal. I tell you— (*she winks and digs Romeo in the ribs*) —he that can lay hold of her shall have the chinks. (*She bustles away.*)

ROMEO   Is she a Capulet? O dear account. My life is my foe's debt!

Aghast at this blow of fortune, Romeo disappears among the dancers. Juliet, having done with her mother, returns.

JULIET   Come hither, Nurse. What's he that is now going out of door?

NURSE   I know not. (*She speaks evasively.*)

JULIET   Go ask his name. If he be married, my grave is like to be my wedding bed.

NURSE   His name is Romeo, and a Montague, the only son of your great enemy.

JULIET   My only love sprung from my only hate! Too early seen unknown, and known too late!

NURSE   What's this? What's this?

JULIET   A rhyme I learned even now, of one I danced withal.

NURSE   (*leading Juliet away*) Anon, anon! Come let's away, the strangers are all gone!

Night. The moon shines brightly on the orchard of the Capulets' house. There is a balcony, like a carved stone pocket, from which Juliet surveys the moonlight.

JULIET   O Romeo, Romeo, wherefore art thou Romeo? Deny thy father and refuse thy name . . . 'Tis but thy name that is my enemy; thou art thyself, though not a Montague. What's in a name? That which we call a rose by any other word would smell as sweet: so Romeo would, were he not Romeo called. Romeo, doff thy name, and for thy name, which is no part of thee, take all myself.

Suddenly, Romeo appears from the shadows and stands below the balcony.

ROMEO   I take thee at thy word! Call me but love and I'll be new baptised: henceforth I never will be Romeo!

JULIET   How cam'st thou hither? The orchard walls are high and hard to climb—

ROMEO   —With love's light wings—

JULIET   —And the place death, considering who thou art, if any of my kinsmen find thee here!

ROMEO   Thy kinsmen are no stop to me!

JULIET   If they do see thee, they will murder thee!

ROMEO   Alack, there lies more peril in thine eye than twenty of their swords! Look thou but sweet and I am proof against their enmity!

JULIET Thou knowest the mask of night is on my face, else would a maiden blush bepaint my cheek for that which thou hast heard me speak tonight. Fain would I deny what I have spoke. But farewell, compliment. Dost thou love me? I know thou wilt say 'Ay', and I will take thy word. O gentle Romeo, if thou dost love, pronounce it faithfully—

ROMEO Lady, by yonder blessed moon I vow—

JULIET O swear not by the moon, the inconstant moon—

ROMEO What shall I swear by?

JULIET Do not swear at all.

ROMEO If my heart's dear love—

JULIET Well, do not swear. Although I joy in thee, I have no joy of this contract tonight: it is too rash, too unadvised, too sudden, too like the lightning, which doth cease to be ere one can say 'It lightens'. Sweet, good night.

ROMEO O wilt thou leave me so unsatisfied?

JULIET What satisfaction canst thou have tonight? I hear some noise within. Dear love, adieu.

NURSE'S VOICE (*from within*) Madam.

JULIET (*to Romeo*) Stay but a little, I will come again. (*She leaves the balcony for her room.*)

ROMEO I am afeard, being in night, all this is but a dream.

Juliet returns.

JULIET Three words, dear Romeo, and good night indeed. If thy bent of love be honourable, thy purpose marriage, send me word tomorrow by one that I'll procure to come to thee, where and what time thou wilt perform the rite, and all my fortunes at thy foot I'll lay . . .

ROMEO How silver-sweet sound lovers' tongues by night . . .

JULIET What o'clock tomorrow shall I send to thee?

ROMEO By the hour of nine.

NURSE (*within*) Madam—

JULIET Anon, good Nurse! Good night, good night. Parting is such sweet sorrow that I shall say good night till it be morrow.

Morning. A busy street. Mercutio and Benvolio are seeking Romeo, calling out his name and shouting up at windows, to the annoyance of those within, most of all to the annoyance of the house of Rosalyne where they strongly suspect Romeo is concealed.

MERCUTIO Where the devil should this Romeo be? Came he not home tonight?

BENVOLIO Not to his father's; I spoke with his man. Tybalt, the kinsman to old Capulet, hath sent a letter to his father's house.

TYBALT A challenge, on my life!

BENVOLIO Romeo will answer it. Here comes Romeo!

Romeo enters, all dreamy softness and smiles.

MERCUTIO You gave us the counterfeit fairly last night.

ROMEO Good morrow to you both. What counterfeit did I give you?

MERCUTIO The slip, sir, the slip!

As they converse, the nurse appears, bustling along the street, preceded by her servant. She is a veritable galleon of a figure.

ROMEO   Here's goodly gear! A sail! A sail!

MERCUTIO   Two. Two. A shirt and a smock!

At once the three friends seize hold of the nurse and twirl her round and round. At length, the foolery subsides. The nurse is panting for breath.

NURSE   Out upon you! Gentlemen, can any of you tell me where I can find the young Romeo? (*Romeo bows in acknowledgement.*) If you be he, sir, I desire some confidence with you.

MERCUTIO   She will invite him to some supper.

Romeo waves his friends away. Mockingly, they bow as they depart.

MERCUTIO   Farewell, ancient lady, farewell . . .

NURSE   (*to Romeo*) Pray you, sir, a word—my young lady bid me
enquire you out. What she bid me say, I will keep to myself.
But first let me tell ye, if ye should lead her into a fool's
paradise, as they say, it were a very gross behaviour, as they
say; for the gentlewoman is young.

ROMEO   Nurse, commend me to thy lady and mistress. Bid her devise
some means to come to shrift this afternoon, and there she
shall at Friar Laurence's cell, be shrived and married.

NURSE   Now God in heaven bless thee. This afternoon, sir? Well, she
shall be there.

In her apartment in the Capulets' house, Juliet waits impatiently for the return of the nurse, alternately pacing the floor and rushing to the window.

JULIET   The clock struck nine when I did send the Nurse, in half an
hour she promised to return. Had she affections and warm
youthful blood she would have been as swift in motion as a
ball. But old folks, many feign as they were dead—unwieldy,
slow, heavy, and pale as lead. O God she comes! (*She flies from
the room to greet the nurse.*) O honey Nurse, what news? Hast
thou met with him?

NURSE   Jesu, what haste. Can you not stay awhile? Do you not see I am
out of breath?

JULIET   How art thou out of breath to say thou art out of breath? Is thy news good or bad?

NURSE   Lord, how my head aches—

JULIET   What says he of our marriage?

NURSE   O God's lady dear, are you so hot?

JULIET   Come, what says Romeo?

NURSE   Have you got leave to go to shrift today?

JULIET   I have.

NURSE   Then hie you hence to Friar Laurence' cell. There stays a husband to make you a wife.

Juliet stares at the nurse, then embraces her wildly.

Friar Laurence's cell. A plain, white-washed room with an altar and crucifix above. The window looks out upon a neat herb garden. Romeo is waiting, in company with the friar, a kindly old man in monkish habit.

FRIAR   So smile the heavens on this holy act that after-hours with sorrow chide us not.

ROMEO   (*impatiently*) Amen, amen. Do thou but close our hands with holy words, then love-devouring death do what he dare—

FRIAR   These violent delights have violent ends— (*he glances through the window*) Here comes the lady.

Juliet enters, as if blown in by the summer breeze. At once, she and Romeo embrace.

FRIAR   Come, come with me and we will make short work, for, by your leaves, you shall not stay alone till holy church incorporate two in one.

He leads them to the altar, where, side by side, they kneel before the friar.

A street, in blazing sunshine, making the shadows sharp as knives. Mercutio and Benvolio are together.

BENVOLIO   I pray thee, good Mercutio, let's retire; the day is hot, the Capel are abroad, and if we meet we shall not 'scape a brawl, for now, these hot days, is the mad blood stirring. (*Even as he speaks, Tybalt and his followers appear.*) By my head, here comes the Capulets!

MERCUTIO   By my heel, I care not.

TYBALT   Gentlemen, good e'en: a word with one of you. Mercutio, thou consortest with Romeo.

MERCUTIO   Consort? What, dost thou make us minstrels?

Mercutio's hand goes to his sword; but, at that moment, Romeo appears in the street. He walks as if on air. He is every inch the new-made bridegroom. He is holding a red rose, doubtless the late property of Juliet.

TYBALT   Peace be with you, sir, here comes my man. (*He addresses the rapturous Romeo.*) Boy, turn and draw. (*He flicks the flower from Romeo's hand with his rapier.*)

ROMEO   I do protest. I never injured thee, but love thee better than thou canst devise—

MERCUTIO   (*outraged*) O calm, dishonourable, vile submission! Tybalt, you ratcatcher! Will you walk?

TYBALT   I am for you! (*Tybalt and Mercutio begin to fight.*)

ROMEO   Gentlemen, for shame! Hold, Tybalt! Good Mercutio!

He tries to pull Mercutio away. Tybalt lunges with his rapier, and pierces Mercutio. Mercutio cries out and Tybalt stares, amazed, at his blood-stained blade.

The Capulets fly from the scene. Mercutio staggers. Romeo makes to support him. Mercutio pushes him away, angrily. He sinks to the ground.

MERCUTIO   I am hurt. A plague o' both your houses. I am sped. Is he gone and hath nothing?

ROMEO   What, art thou hurt?

MERCUTIO   Ay, ay, a scratch, a scratch. Marry, 'tis enough.

ROMEO   Courage, man, the hurt cannot be much.

MERCUTIO   No, 'tis not so deep as a well, nor so wide as a church door, but 'tis enough. Ask for me tomorrow and you shall find me a grave man. I am peppered, I warrant, for this world. A plague o' both your houses. Why the devil came you between us? I was hurt under your arm.

ROMEO   I thought all for the best.

MERCUTIO   A plague o' both your houses! They have made worm's meat of me . . .

Mercutio dies. As Romeo looks down, shamed by his friend's reproach and grief-stricken by his death, a shadow falls across the body of Mercutio. Romeo looks up. Tybalt has returned. Enraged, Romeo draws his sword. They fight. Tybalt is killed.

Romeo stares in horror at what he has done. A crowd begins to gather. Benvolio seizes Romeo by the arm.

BENVOLIO   Romeo, away, be gone! The Prince will doom thee to death!

ROMEO   O, I am fortune's fool!

Romeo flies for his life.

Night. Friar Laurence's cell. The door opens. The good friar enters, bearing a lantern that casts wild shadows.

FRIAR   Romeo, come forth, come forth, thou fearful man.

Romeo emerges palely from the shadows.

ROMEO   Father, what news? What is the Prince's doom?

FRIAR   A gentler judgement vanished from his lips: not body's death, but body's banishment. Hence from Verona art thou banished—

ROMEO   'Tis torture and not mercy! Heaven is here where Juliet lives, and every cat and dog and little mouse, every unworthy thing lives here in heaven and may look on her, but Romeo may not—

FRIAR Thou fond mad man, hear me a little speak— (*There is a knocking on the door.*) Who's there?

NURSE'S VOICE I come from Lady Juliet.

The nurse enters.

ROMEO Nurse!

NURSE Ah sir, ah sir, death's the end of all.

ROMEO Spak'st thou of Juliet? How is it with her? Doth not she think me an old murderer now I have stained the childhood of our joy with blood removed but little from her own?

NURSE O, she says nothing, sir, but weeps and weeps, and now falls on her bed, and then starts up, and Tybalt calls, and then on Romeo cries, and then down falls again.

Romeo draws his dagger as if to kill himself.

FRIAR Hold thy desperate hand. Go, get thee to thy love as was decreed, ascend her chamber—hence, and comfort her. But look thou stay not till the Watch be set, for then thou canst not pass to Mantua where thou shalt live till we can find a time to blaze your marriage, reconcile your friends, beg pardon of the Prince and call thee back . . .

NURSE Hie you, make haste, for it grows very late.

FRIAR Go hence, good night: either be gone before the Watch is set, or by the break of day . . .

Juliet's balcony. The night is giving way to a ragged grey dawn. A lark begins to sing. Romeo comes out of the bedchamber onto the balcony. Juliet follows . . .

JULIET Wilt thou be gone? It is not yet near day, it was the nightingale and not the lark—

ROMEO It was the lark, the herald of the morn. Look, love, night's candles are burnt out, and jocund day stands tiptoe on the misty mountain tops. I must be gone and live, or stay and die.

JULIET   Yond light is not daylight, I know it—

ROMEO   Come death, and welcome. Juliet wills it so. It is not day—

JULIET   It is, it is. Hie hence, begone, away. It is the lark that sings so out of tune—

NURSE'S VOICE   Madam, your lady mother is coming to your chamber. The day is broke, be wary, look about.

Romeo and Juliet embrace passionately; then Romeo descends a rope ladder that hangs from the balcony.

ROMEO   Farewell, farewell.

Juliet stares down into the darkness in which Romeo's face gleams palely, like a drowned man.

JULIET   O think'st thou we shall ever meet again?

ROMEO   I doubt it not—

JULIET   O God, I have an ill-divining soul! Methinks I see thee, now thou art so low, as one dead in the bottom of a tomb.

ROMEO   Adieu, adieu!

With a last wave, he vanishes. Juliet stares vainly for another glimpse of him. Lady Capulet enters the bedchamber. Juliet hastily leaves the balcony and returns inside.

LADY CAPULET	Why, how now, Juliet?
JULIET	Madam, I am not well.
LADY CAPULET	Evermore weeping for your cousin's death? Well, well, thou hast a careful father, child; one who to put thee from heaviness hath sorted out a day of sudden joy—
JULIET	What day is that?
LADY CAPULET	Marry, my child, early next Thursday morn the gallant, young and noble gentleman, the County Paris, at Saint Peter's Church, shall happily make thee there a joyful bride!
JULIET	(*aghast*) Now by Saint Peter's Church, and Peter too, he shall not make me there a happy bride! I will not marry yet. And when I do, I swear it shall be Romeo, whom you know I hate, rather than Paris—
LADY CAPULET	Here comes your father, tell him so yourself.

CAPULET	How now, wife, have you delivered to her our decree?
LADY CAPULET	Ay sir, but she will have none.
CAPULET	How? Will she none? Does she not give us thanks? (*He turns, furiously, upon his daughter*) Mistress minion you, but fettle your fine joints 'gainst Thursday next to go with Paris to Saint Peter's Church, or I will drag thee on a hurdle thither. Out, you green-sickness carrion! Out, you baggage!

JULIET   (*kneeling*) Good father, I beseech you—

CAPULET   Hang thee, young baggage, disobedient wretch! I tell thee
            what—get thee to church a Thursday or never after look me in
            the face! (*He storms out, followed by Lady Capulet.*)

JULIET   O God!—O Nurse, comfort me, counsel me!

NURSE   I think it best you married with the County. O, he's a lovely
            gentleman. Romeo's a dishclout to him.

JULIET   (*drawing away from the nurse and staring at her bitterly*) Well,
            thou hast comforted me marvellous much. Go in, and tell my
            lady I am gone, having displeased my father, to Laurence' cell,
            to make confession and be absolved.

NURSE   Marry, I will, and this is wisely done. (*She departs.*)

JULIET   Ancient damnation! O most wicked fiend! Thou and my
            bosom shall henceforth be twain. I'll to the Friar to know his
            remedy; if all else fail, myself have power to die.

In Friar Laurence's cell. Juliet kneels before the friar.

JULIET   God joined my heart and Romeo's, thou our hands; and ere
            this hand, by thee to Romeo sealed, or my true heart with
            treacherous revolt turn to another, this shall slay them both.
            (*She takes a dagger from her bosom.*)

FRIAR   Hold, daughter. I do spy a kind of hope. Go home, be merry,
            give consent to marry Paris. Wednesday is tomorrow;
            tomorrow night look that thou lie alone. Let not the Nurse lie
            with thee in thy chamber. (*He takes a small bottle from a shelf
            and gives it to her.*) Take thou this vial, being then in bed, and
            this distilling liquor drink thou off . . . Now when the
            bridegroom in the morning comes to rouse thee from thy bed,
            there thou art, dead. Then as the manner of our country is, in
            thy best robes, thou shalt be borne to that same ancient vault
            where all the kindred of the Capulets lie. In this borrowed
            likeness of shrunk death thou shalt continue two and forty
            hours and then awake as from a pleasant sleep. In the mean-
            time, against thou shalt awake, shall Romeo by my letters

know our drift and hither shall he come, and he and I will watch thy waking, and that very night shall Romeo bear thee hence to Mantua.

Juliet nods and, clutching the vial, departs. Hastily, Friar Laurence writes a letter and summons Friar John, a brother of his order, to take the letter to Romeo in Mantua.

A street in Mantua. Romeo waits, his eyes never leaving the road that leads to Verona. A horseman appears and rides towards him. It is his servant.

ROMEO News from Verona! How doth my lady? Is my father well? How doth my Juliet? That I ask again, for nothing can be ill if she be well!

SERVANT	Then she is well and nothing can be ill. Her body sleeps in Capels' monument. I saw her laid low in her kindred's vault. O pardon me for bringing you these ill news.
ROMEO	Is it e'en so? (*The servant nods.*) Then I defy you, stars! I will hence tonight!
SERVANT	I do beseech you, sir, have patience!
ROMEO	Leave me. Hast thou no letters to me from the Friar?
SERVANT	None, my good lord.
ROMEO	No matter. Get thee gone. (*The servant leaves him.*) Well, Juliet, I will lie with thee tonight. Let's see for means. O mischief thou art swift to enter in the thoughts of desperate men. I do remember an apothecary . . .

The apothecary's shop. 'In his needy shop a tortoise hung, an alligator stuffed, and other skins of ill-shaped fishes; and about his shelves a beggarly account of empty boxes, green earthenware pots, bladders and musty seeds, remnants of packthread, and old cakes of roses . . .' Romeo enters, and the apothecary comes to attend him: 'in tattered weeds, with overwhelming brows.' Romeo leans upon the counter and beckons.

ROMEO   Come hither, man. I see thou art poor. There is forty ducats.
Let me have a dram of poison.

APOTHECARY   Such mortal drugs I have, but Mantua's law is death to any he
that utters them.

ROMEO   Art thou so bare and full of wretchedness, and fear'st to die?
The world is not thy friend, nor the world's law; the world
affords no law to make thee rich; then be not poor, but break
it, and take this. (*He pushes the money across the counter.*)

APOTHECARY   (*staring at the money*) My poverty, but not my will consents.

ROMEO   I pay thy poverty and not thy will.

*The apothecary fumbles on his shelves and takes down a vial,
which he lays on the counter. The withered hand of the
apothecary and the fine white hand of Romeo cross: one takes
the gold, the other, the poison.*

ROMEO   I sell thee poison, thou hast sold me none. Farewell, buy food,
get thyself in flesh.

He hastens from the shop.

Friar Laurence's cell. Friar Laurence looks up from his studies as Friar John enters.

FRIAR LAURENCE   Friar John, welcome from Mantua. What says Romeo?

Friar John gravely shakes his head.

FRIAR JOHN   Going to find a barefoot brother out, one of our order, to associate me, here in this city visiting the sick, and finding him, the searchers of the town, suspecting that we both were in a house where the infectious pestilence did reign, sealed up the doors and would not let us forth, so that my speed to Mantua there was stayed.

FRIAR LAURENCE   Who bare my letter then to Romeo?

FRIAR JOHN   I could not send it—here it is again—

FRIAR LAURENCE   Unhappy fortune! Now must I to the monument alone! Within these three hours will the fair Juliet wake!

In the utmost agitation, he leaves the cell; then, a moment later, returns for his lantern. He rushes forth again, and Friar John, full of guilt, watches Friar Laurence, lit by his lantern, whirl off into the dark . . .

Within the monument of the Capulets. Juliet lies motionless on her bier, illuminated by four tall candles. About her, in the shadowy gloom, lie broken coffins on shelves . . . some with bones protruding and skulls peeping inquisitively forth, as if to welcome their fair new neighbour. Romeo enters. He approaches Juliet, and kneels beside her.

ROMEO   O my love, my wife! Death that hath sucked the honey of thy breath hath had no power upon thy beauty yet. Thou art not conquered. Beauty's ensign yet is crimson on thy lips and in thy cheeks, and Death's pale flag is not advanced there. Here, here will I remain with worms that are thy chambermaids; O here will I set up my everlasting rest . . . Eyes look your last! Arms take your last embrace! And lips, O you the doors of breath, seal with a righteous kiss a dateless bargain with engrossing Death!

He kisses Juliet, then holds up the vial of poison like a glass of wine.

ROMEO   Here's to my love! (*He drinks.*) O true Apothecary, thy drugs are quick!

He kisses Juliet again, then dies. A moment later, Friar Laurence enters the tomb. He gazes in despair at the scene. Slowly, Juliet stirs. She sees the friar.

JULIET   O comfortable Friar, where is my lord? (*She stares about her at the images of death and decay.*) I do remember well where I should be, and there I am. Where is my Romeo?

FRIAR   I hear some noise. Lady, come from that nest of death, contagion, and unnatural sleep. A greater power than we can contradict hath thwarted our intents. Come, come away! Thy husband in thy bosom there lies dead. Come, I'll dispose of thee among a sisterhood of holy nuns. Stay not to question, for the Watch is coming. Come, go, good Juliet. I dare no longer stay.

JULIET   (*with quiet dignity*) Go, get thee hence, for I will not away.

The friar, wringing his hands in grief and dismay, departs. Juliet rises, and kneels beside the dead Romeo. She takes his hand and discovers the vial, still clutched in it.

JULIET   What's here? A cup closed in my true love's hand? Poison, I see, hath been his timeless end. (*She takes it, and sees it to be empty.*) O churl. Drunk all, and left no friendly drop to help me after? I will kiss thy lips. Haply some poison yet doth hang on them. (*She kisses him.*) Thy lips are warm—

There are sounds of people approaching: shouts and cries as they approach the tomb.

JULIET   Yea, a noise? Then I'll be brief. (*She takes Romeo's dagger.*)
O happy dagger. This is thy sheath. There rust, and let me die.
(*She stabs herself and falls lifeless into the arms of the dead
Romeo.*)

*Figures come crowding into the tomb, flourishing torches.
Among the awed faces are old Capulet and Montague. Then
comes the Prince. He surveys the tragic scene, and turns to the
bereaved parents.*

PRINCE   Capulet, Montague, see what a scourge is laid upon your hate,
that heaven finds means to kill your joys with love . . .

CAPULET   O brother Montague, give me thy hand. This is my daughter's
jointure, for no more can I demand.

MONTAGUE   But I can give thee more, for I will raise her statue in pure gold,
that whiles Verona by that name is known, there shall no figure
at such rate be set as that of true and faithful Juliet.

CAPULET   As rich shall Romeo's by his lady lie, poor sacrifices to our enmity.

The curtain falls, not on the darkness of the lovers' tomb, but on the brightness of it.